HAL•LEONARD DRUM PLAY-ALONG

Motown

VOL.

CONTENTS

Tracking, mixing, and mastering by
Jake Johnson & Bill Maynard at Paradyme Productions
Drums by Scott Schroedl
Guitars by Doug Boduch
Bass by Tom McGirr
Keyboards by Warren Wiegratz

ISBN 978-1-4234-4660-6

HAL•LEONARD® CORPORATION

7777 W. BLUEMOUND RD. P.O. BOX 13819 MILWAUKEE, WI 53213

Visit Hal Leonard Online at
www.halleonard.com

Ain't Too Proud to Beg

Words and Music by Edward Holland and Norman Whitfield

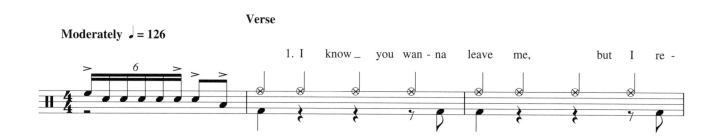

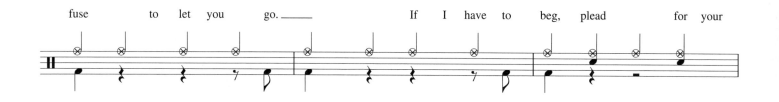

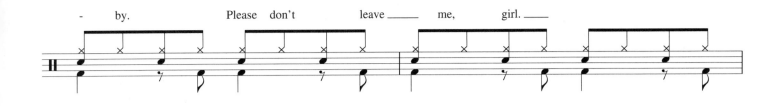

- by.   Please don't   leave _____ me,   girl. _____

𝄋 Verse

2. Now, I've heard _____ a cry - in' man ___ is half __ a man, ___ with
3., 4. *See additional lyrics*

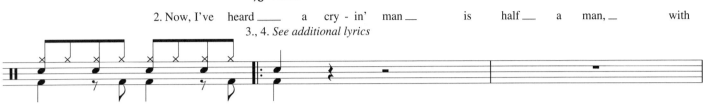

no   sense of pride. _____   But if I have to   cry   to keep __ you,   I

don't mind _____ weep - in' if it - 'll   keep   you   by   my   side. _____

Chorus

3rd time, substitute Fill 1

___   Ain't __ too   proud _____ to   beg,   you   know __

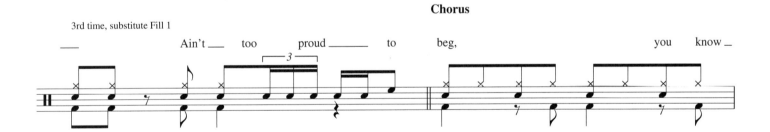

__ it.   Please don't   leave __ me, girl, ___   Ain't too proud   to

Fill 1

3

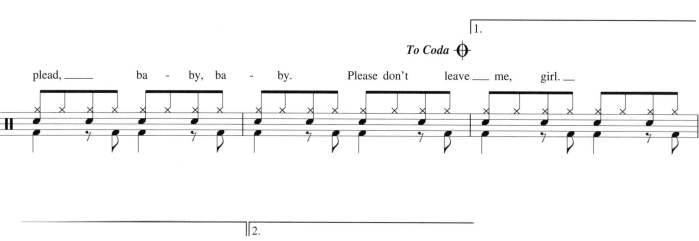

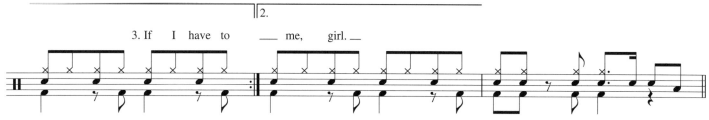

Sax Solo

D.S. al Coda

Play 7 times

Coda

Begin fade

Fade out

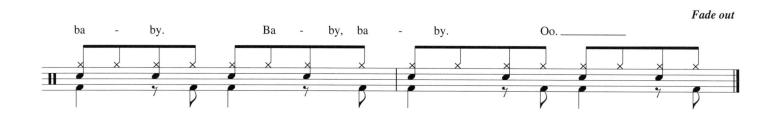

Additional Lyrics

3. If I have to sleep on your doorstep all night and day
   Just to keep you from walking away.
   Let your friends laugh, even this I can stand,
   'Cause I wanna keep you any way I can.

4. Now, I've got a love so deep in the pit of my heart,
   And each day it grows more and more.
   I'm not ashamed to call and plead to you, baby,
   If pleading keeps you from walking out that door.

Dancing in the Street

Words and Music by Marvin Gaye, Ivy Hunter and William Stevenson

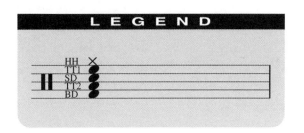

Intro
Moderately ♩ = 114

Verse
1. Call - ing out __ a - round __

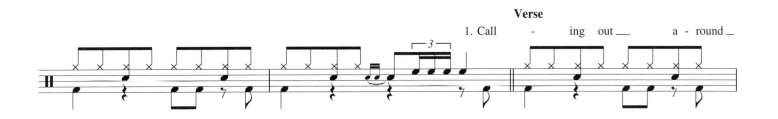

__ the world, __ are you read - y for a brand new beat? __

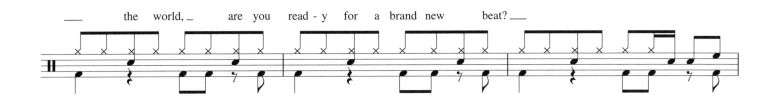

Sum - mer's here __ and the time is right __ for danc - ing __ in the street. __

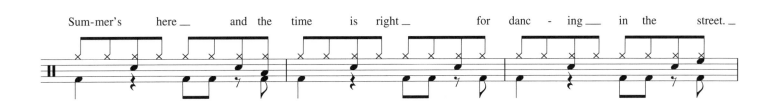

__ They're danc - ing in Chi - ca - go, __ down in

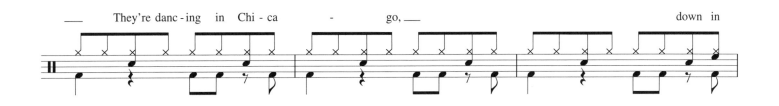

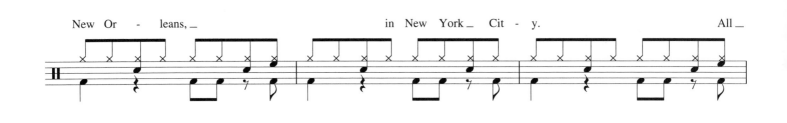

New Or - leans, _ in New York _ Cit - y. All _

_ we need ____ is mu - sic, sweet __ mu -

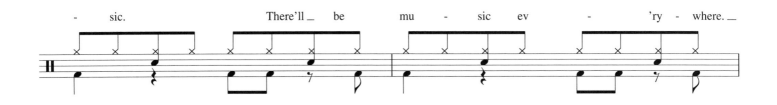

- sic. There'll _ be mu - sic ev - 'ry - where. _

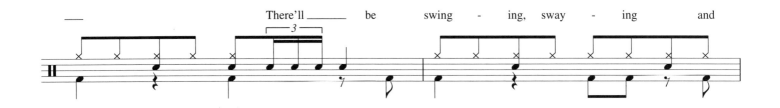

_ There'll ____ be swing - ing, sway - ing and

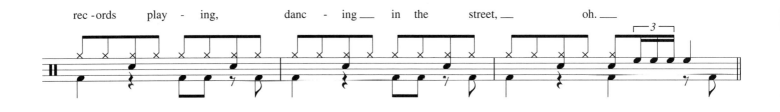

rec - ords play - ing, danc - ing __ in the street, _ oh. _

Chorus

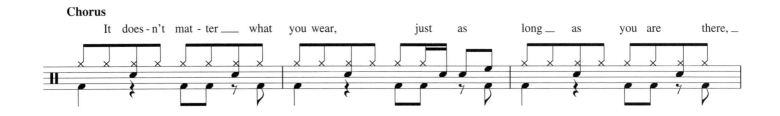

It does - n't mat - ter __ what you wear, just as long _ as you are there, _

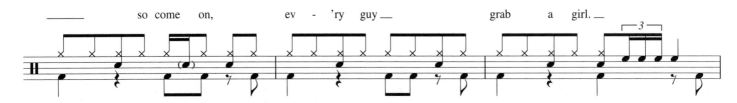

____ so come on, ev - 'ry guy _ grab a girl. _

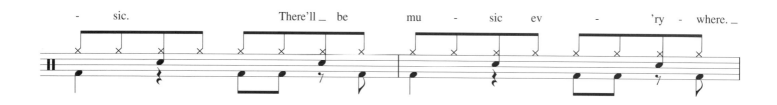

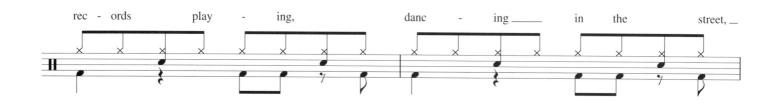

Chorus

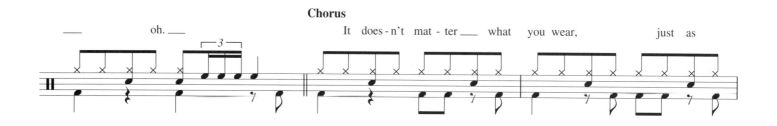

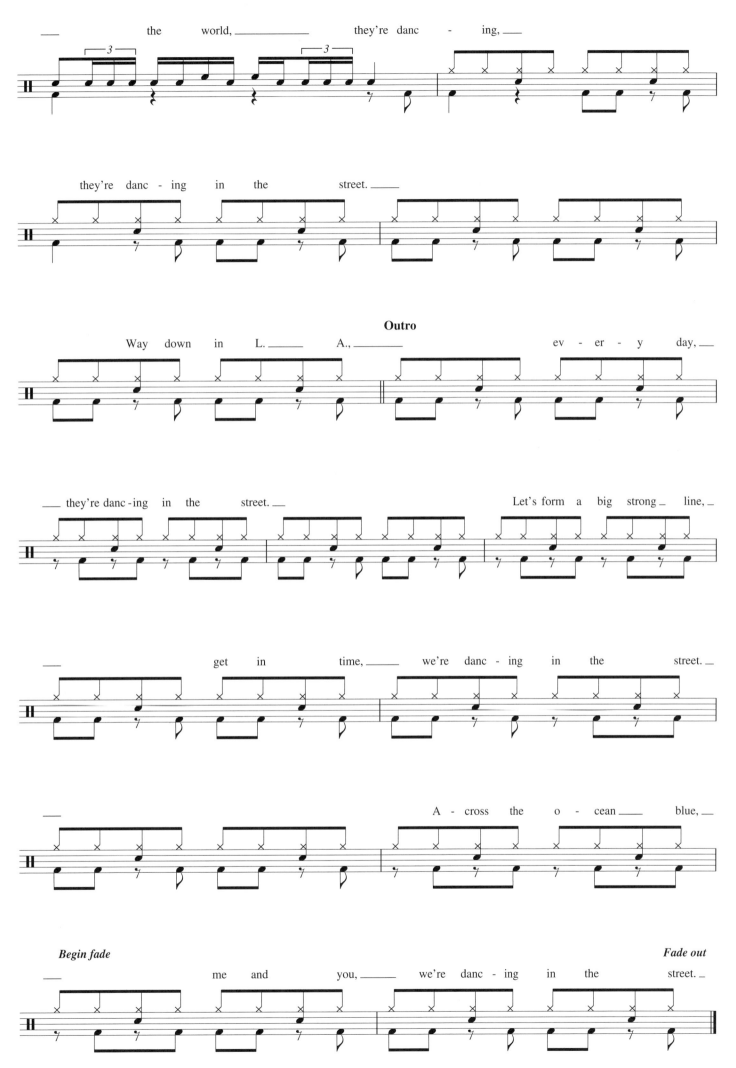

Get Ready

Words and Music by William "Smokey" Robinson

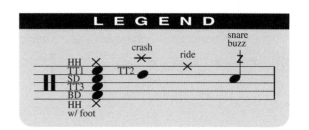

tell them you do.   You're out-ta   sight.   Well, twee-dle-e-dee, __

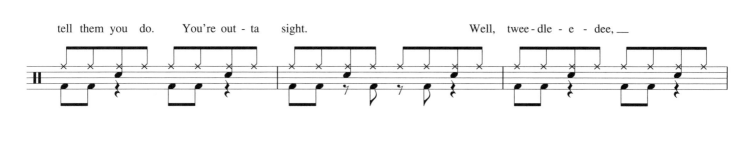

twee-dle-e-dum. __   Look out,   ba - by,   'cause here I   come. __

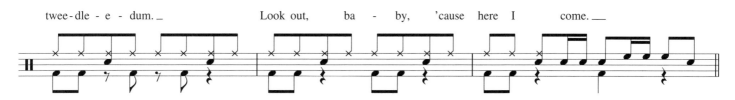

Chorus

I'm bring-in' you a   love that's true. __   (Get   read-y,   get

read - y.)   I'll start mak-in' love   to you.   Get

read - y,   get   read - y.   (Get   read-y,   'cause

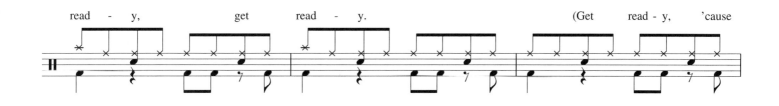

here I   come. __   Get   read-y, 'cause here I   come.) __   2. You

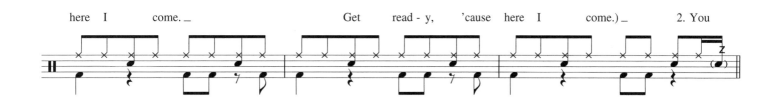

Verse

wan-na play hide __ and   seek __ with   love, __   let me re-mind__ ya,

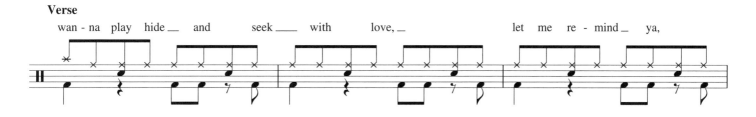

lov - in', you're gon - na miss

and the time it takes to find _____ ya.

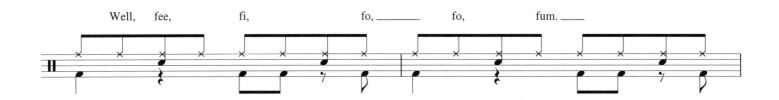

Well, fee, fi, fo, _____ fo, fum. ___

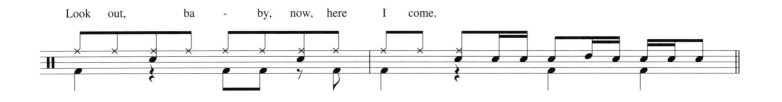

Look out, ba - by, now, here I come.

Chorus

I'm bring - in' you a love that's true. ___ (Get read - y, get

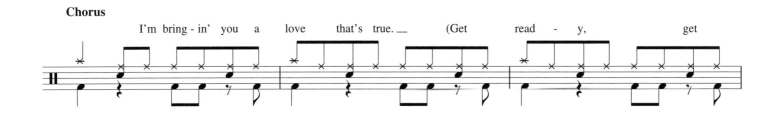

read - y.) I'll start mak - in' love to you. Get

read - y, get read - y. (Get read - y, 'cause

here I   come. __   Get   read - y,   'cause   here I   come.) __

Saxophone Solo

3. If   all ____

Verse

_____ my   friends ____   should - n't   want   me   to,   I   think

I'll   un - der - stand. __   Hope I   get   to   you   be   -   fore __

__ they   do, __   'cause   that's   how   I   planned __   it.

Sir Duke

Words and Music by Stevie Wonder

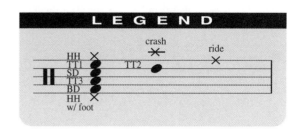

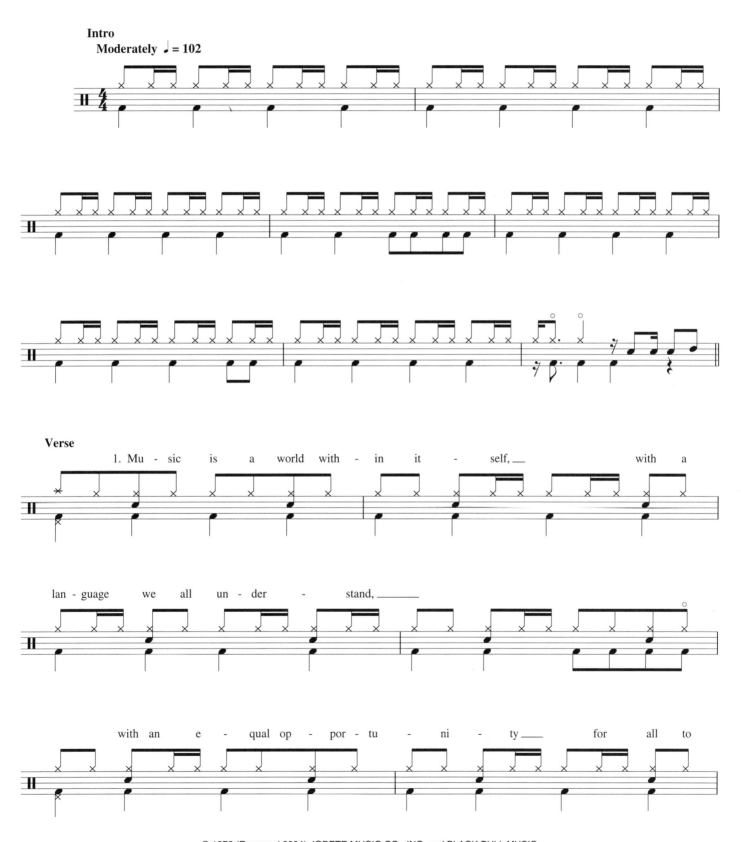

sing, ____ dance and clap their ____ hands. _____ But just be -

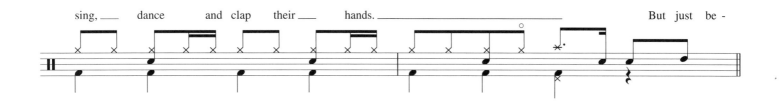

Pre-Chorus

cause a rec - ord has a groove __ don't make it in the groove. __ But you can

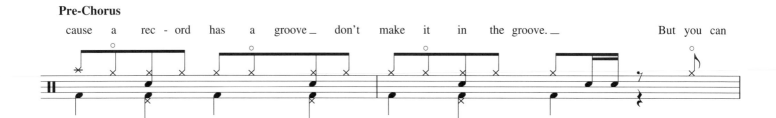

tell right a - way at let - ter A _____ when the peo - ple start to move.

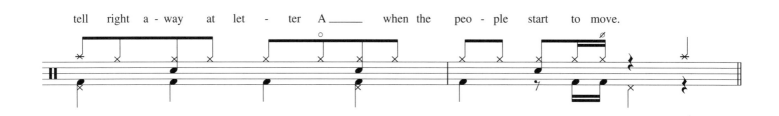

Chorus

They can feel it all _____ o - ver. _____

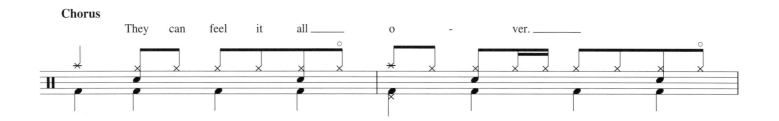

They can feel it all _____ o - ver _____ peo - ple. _____

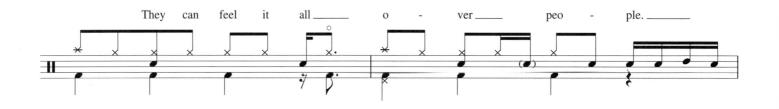

They can feel it all _____ o - ver. _____

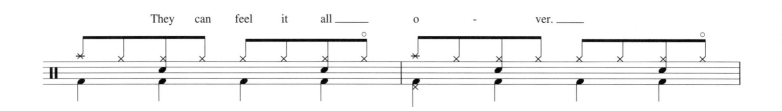

They can feel it all _____ o - ver _____ peo - ple, go!

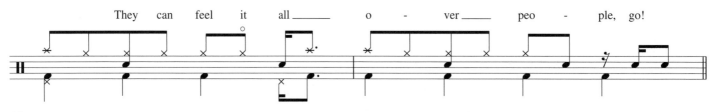

Interlude

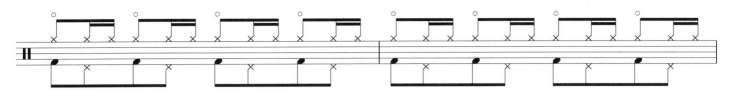

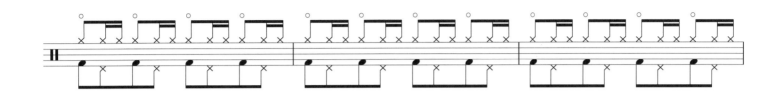

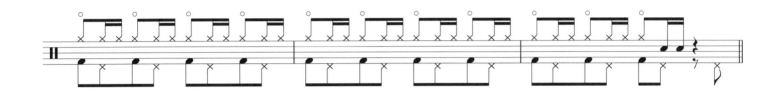

Verse

2. Mu - sic knows ___ it is, ___ and al - ways will be, one of

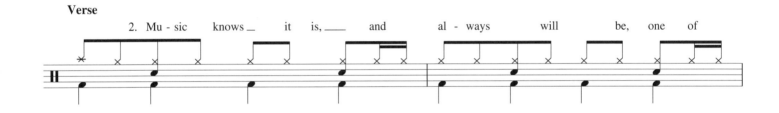

the things that life just won't ___ quit. _____

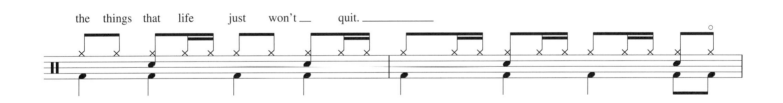

But here are some ___ of mu - sic's pi - o - neers, that time will

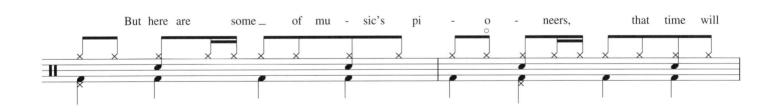

not al - low ___ us to for - get, _____ now. ___ Well, there's

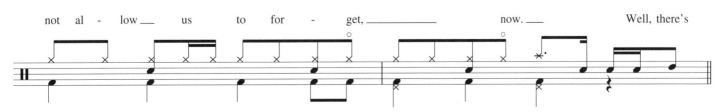

Pre-Chorus

Ba - sie, Mil - ler, Satch - a - mo, __ and the king of all, __ Sir __ Duke. And with a

voice like El - la's ring - in' out, __ there's no way the band __ can lose.

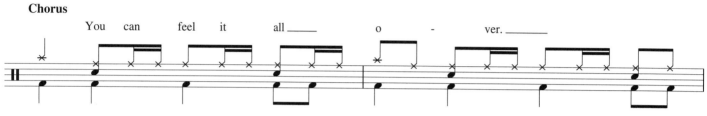

Chorus

You can feel it all ____ o - ver. ____

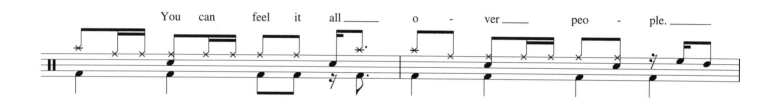

You can feel it all ____ o - ver ___ peo - ple. ____

You can feel it all ____ o - ver. ____

You can feel it all ____ o - ver ___ peo - ple. ____

You can feel it all ____ o - ver. ____

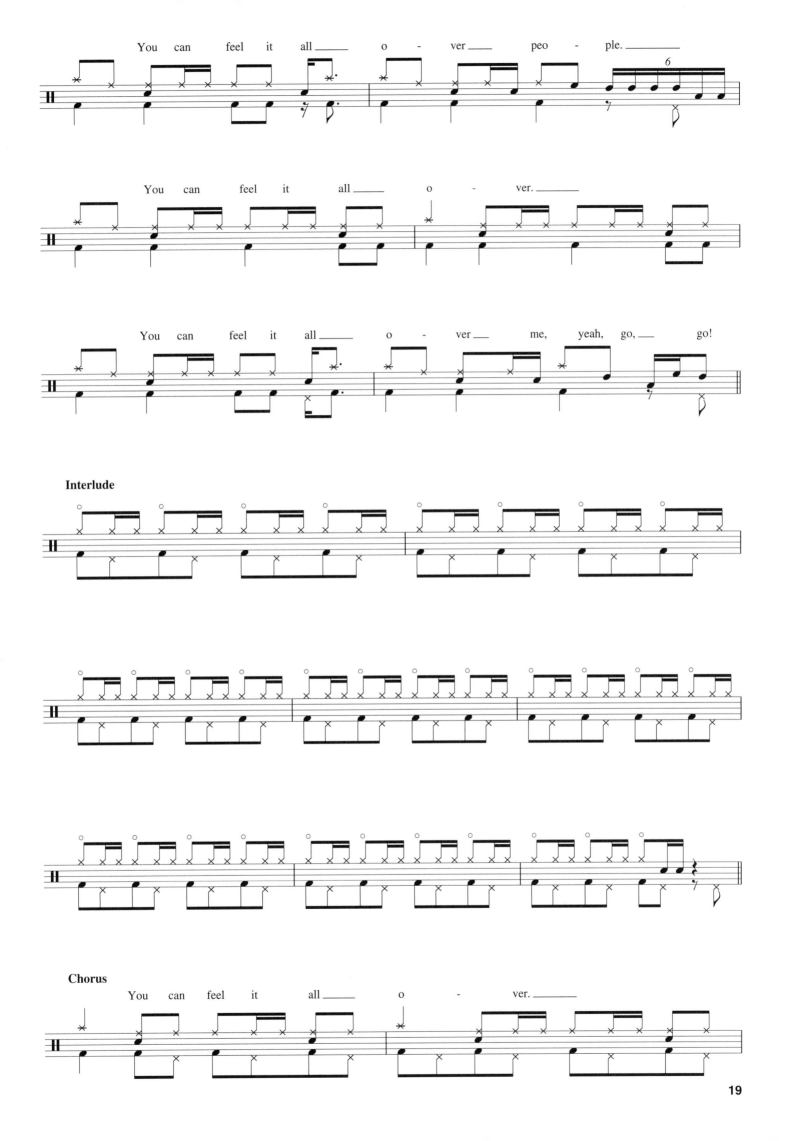

Interlude

Chorus

You can feel it all _____ o - ver. _____

You can feel it all _____ o - ver _____ peo - ple. _____

You can feel it all _____ o - ver. _____

You can feel it all _____ o - ver _____ peo - ple, go!

Outro

How Sweet It Is
(To Be Loved by You)

Words and Music by Edward Holland, Lamont Dozier and Brian Holland

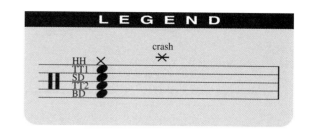

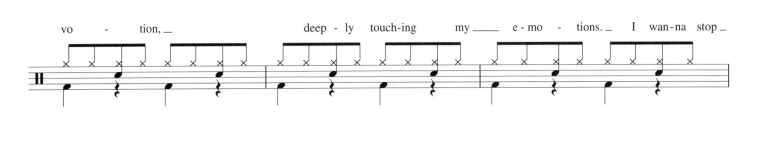

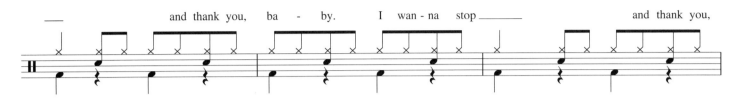

Chorus

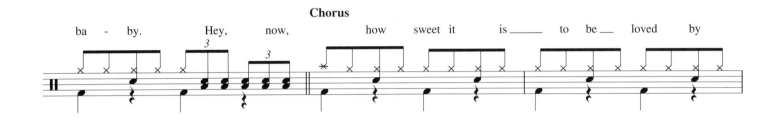

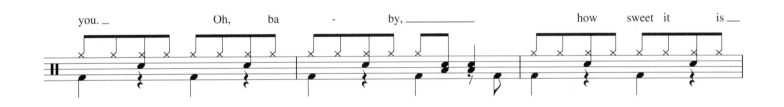

Verse

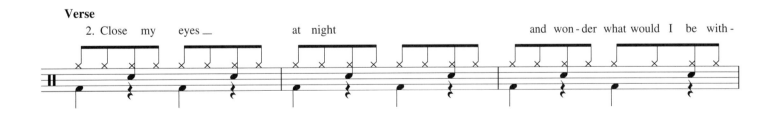

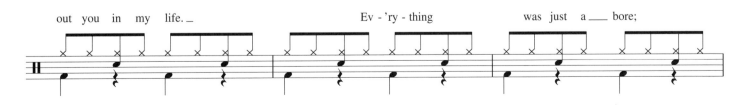

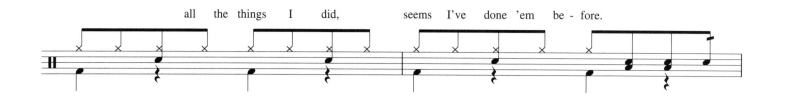

all the things I did, seems I've done 'em be - fore.

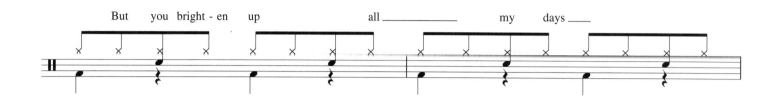

But you bright - en up all _____ my days ___

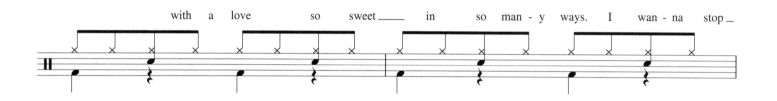

with a love so sweet ___ in so man - y ways. I wan - na stop _

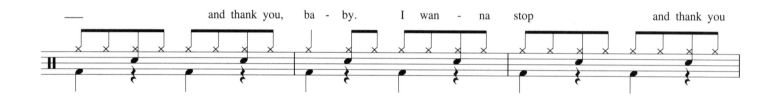

___ and thank you, ba - by. I wan - na stop and thank you

Chorus

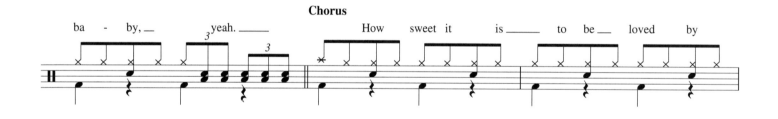

ba - by, __ yeah. ___ How sweet it is ___ to be __ loved by

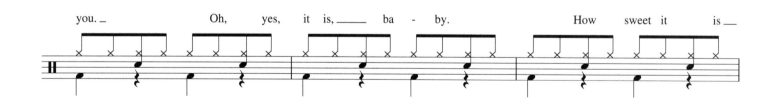

you. _ Oh, yes, it is, ___ ba - by. How sweet it is __

_ to be _ loved _ by you. _ Yes, it is, ba - by, hmm. _

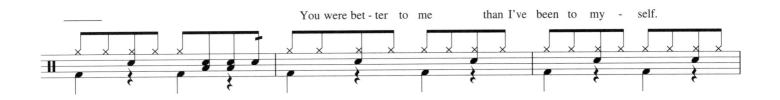

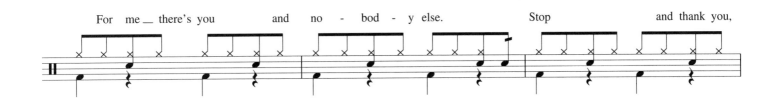

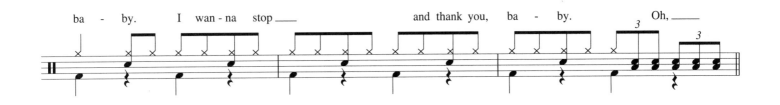

Outro

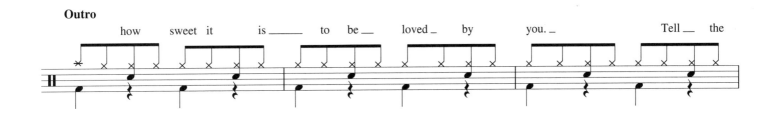

Begin fade

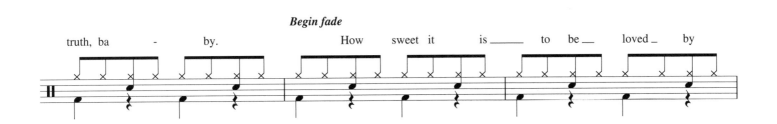

Fade out

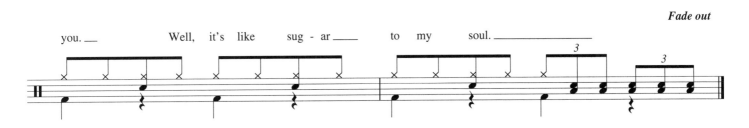

I Can't Help Myself
(Sugar Pie, Honey Bunch)

Words and Music by Brian Holland, Lamont Dozier and Edward Holland

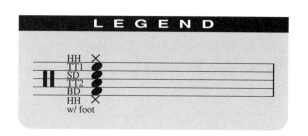

you come and you go, _____   leav - ing _____ just _____ your

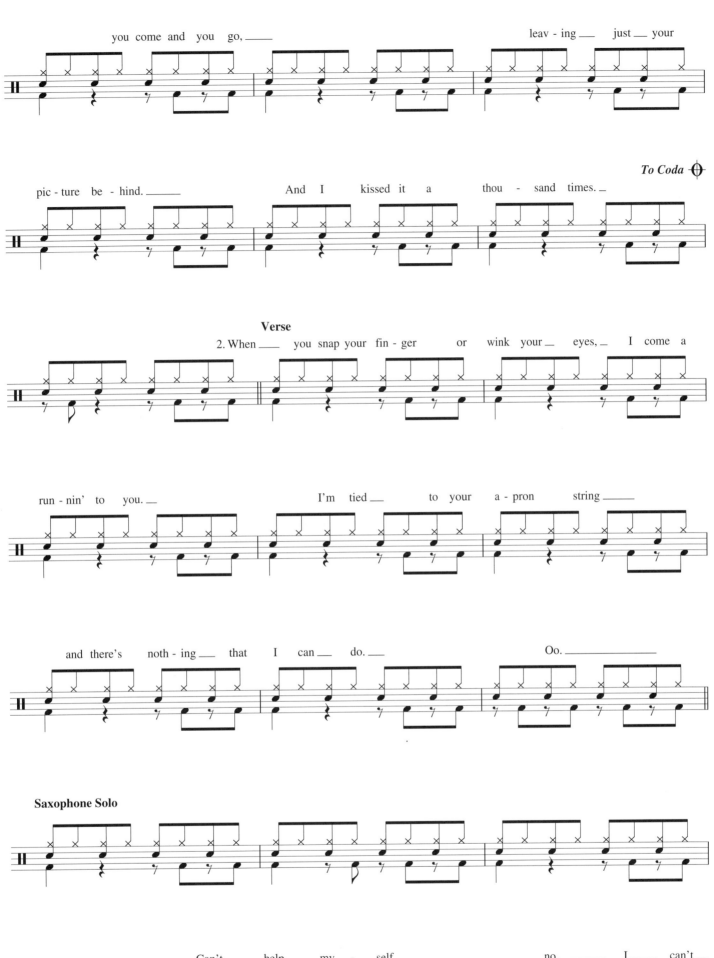

To Coda ⊕

pic - ture be - hind. _____   And   I   kissed it   a   thou - sand times. _____

Verse

2. When _____ you snap your fin - ger   or   wink your _____ eyes, _____ I   come a

run - nin' to   you. _____   I'm   tied _____   to   your   a - pron   string _____

and there's   noth - ing _____ that   I   can _____ do. _____   Oo. _____

Saxophone Solo

Can't   help   my - self, _____   no, _____ I _____ can't _____

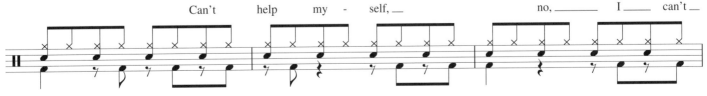

Verse

___ help my - self.   3. 'Cause   sug - ar pie   hon - ey bunch.

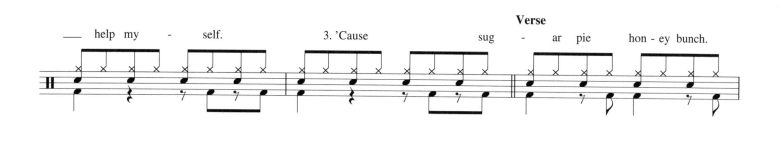

I'm weak - er than a   man   should be. ___   I can't

help   my - self. ___   I'm a fool ___ in ___   love, _ you see. ___

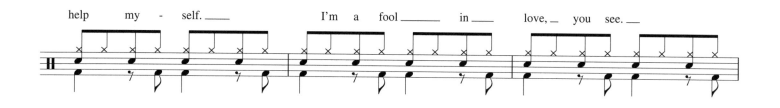

Wan - na tell ___ you I don't love you,   tell ___ you that we're through.

and I've   tried, _   but ev - 'ry time _ I   see your   face ___

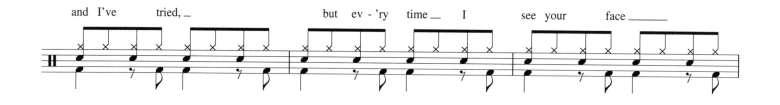

I   get all ___   choked   up in - side. _   When _

Interlude

___ I call your name,   girl, ___ it starts to flame. (Burn - in' in my heart,   tear'n' _

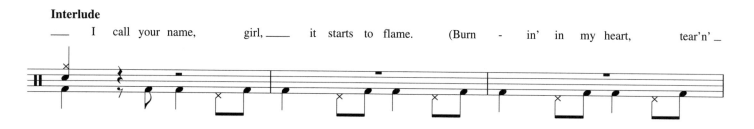

___ it all a - part.) No mat - ter how I try, my love ___ I can-not hide. 4. 'Cause

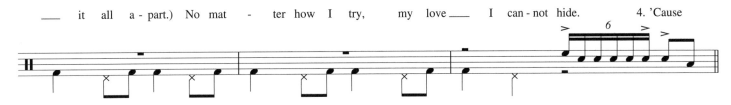

✛ **Coda**

Verse

5. Sug - ar pie hon - ey bunch,

you know that I ___ love you. ___ Can't

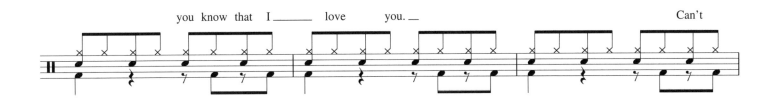

Begin fade

help my - self, no, ___ I can't help my - self. ___

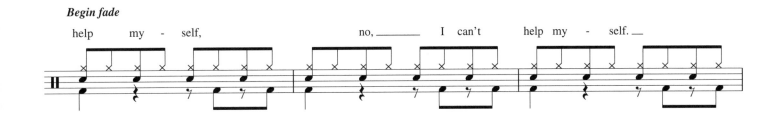

Fade out

Oo. ___ Sug - ar pie hon - ey bunch. (Sug - ar pie hon - ey bunch.)

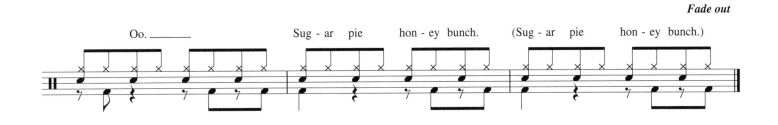

Additional Lyrics

4. 'Cause sugar pie honey bunch,
   You know that I'm waitin' for you.
   Can't help myself,
   I love you and nobody else.
   Sugar pie honey bunch,
   Do anything you ask me to.
   Can't help myself,
   I want you and nobody else.

Stop! In the Name of Love

Words and Music by Lamont Dozier, Brian Holland and Edward Holland

leav-ing me a - lone and hurt. Af - ter I've _ been

good to you. _ Af - ter I've _ been sweet _ to you. _

Chorus

Stop in the name of love, be - fore you

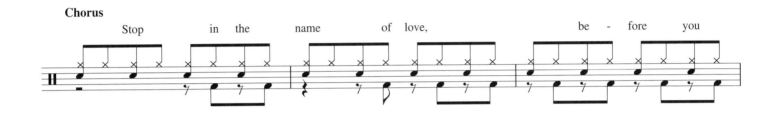

break my heart. Stop in the name of love,

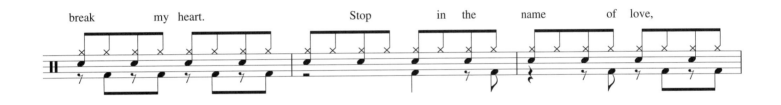

be - fore you break my heart. Think it o - ver.

Think it o - ver.

Verse

2. I've known of your, your se - clud - ed nights, I've e - ven seen her

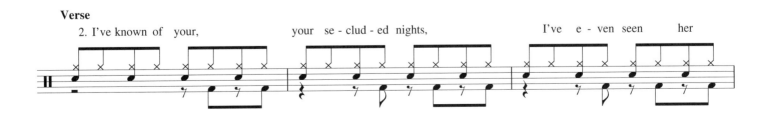

may - be once or twice.   But is   her   sweet   ex - pres - sion

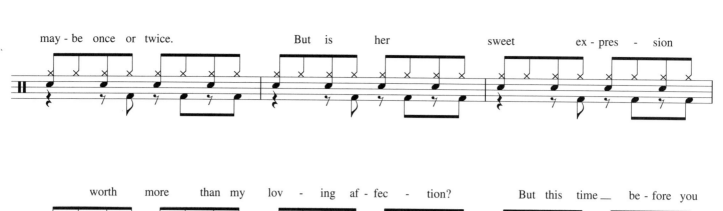

worth   more   than my   lov - ing af - fec - tion?   But this time   be - fore you

leave   my   arms,   and   rush   off   to   her charms.

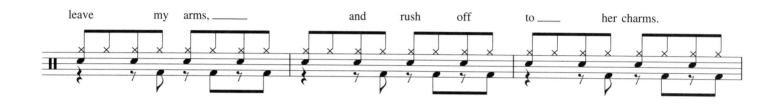

Have-n't I   been good   to you?   Have-n't I   been

Chorus

sweet   to   you? _   Stop   in the   name   of love,

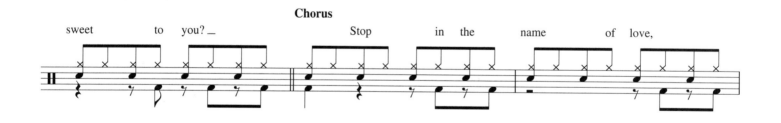

be - fore   you   break   my heart.   Stop   in the

name   of love,   be - fore   you   break   my heart. Think it

o - ver.   Think it o - ver.

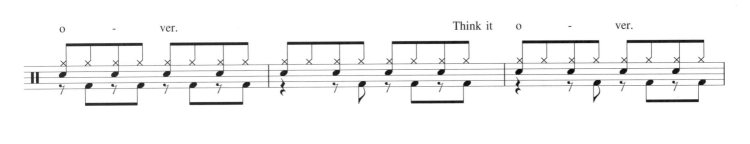

Verse

3. I've tried so hard,   hard to be pa - tient,

hop - ing you'll stop   this in - fat - u - a - tion.   But each __ time __

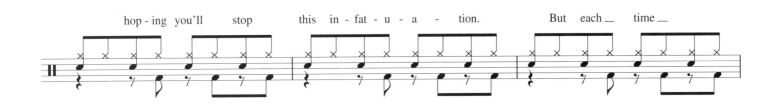

you   are to - geth - er, ___   I'm so a - fraid __ of   los - ing you for - ev - er. ___

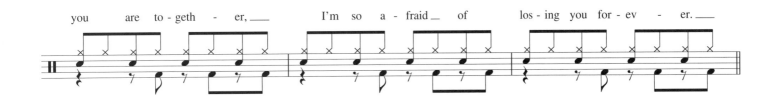

Outro-Chorus

Stop   in the   name   of love,   be - fore   you

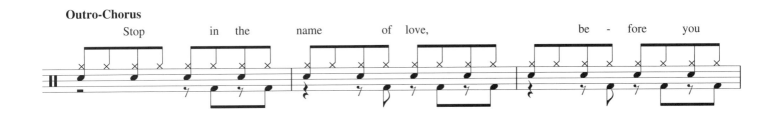

break   my heart.   Stop   in the   name   of love,

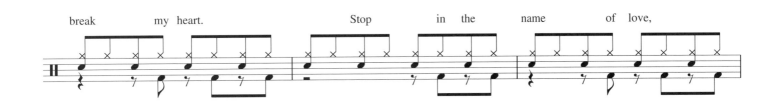

Begin fade   *Fade out*

be - fore   you   break   my heart.   Stop   in the...

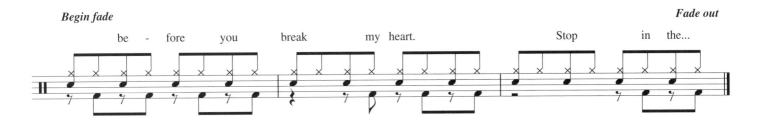

You've Really Got a Hold on Me

Words and Music by William "Smokey" Robinson

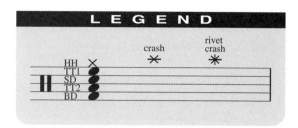

HAL•LEONARD DRUM PLAY-ALONG

Play your favorite songs quickly and easily with the *Drum Play-Along*™ series. Just follow the drum notation, listen to the CD to hear how the drums should sound, then play along using the separate backing tracks. The lyrics are also included for quick reference. The audio CD is playable on any CD player. For PC and Mac computer users, the CD is enhanced so you can adjust the recording to any tempo without changing the pitch!

1. Pop/Rock
Hurts So Good • Message in a Bottle • No Reply at All • Owner of a Lonely Heart • Peg • Rosanna • Separate Ways (Worlds Apart) • Swingtown.
00699742 Book/CD Pack $12.95

2. Classic Rock
Barracuda • Come Together • Mississippi Queen • Radar Love • Space Truckin' • Walk This Way • White Room • Won't Get Fooled Again.
00699741 Book/CD Pack $12.95

3. Hard Rock
Bark at the Moon • Detroit Rock City • Living After Midnight • Panama • Rock You like a Hurricane • Run to the Hills • Smoke on the Water • War Pigs (Interpolating Luke's Wall).
00699743 Book/CD Pack $12.95

4. Modern Rock
Chop Suey! • Duality • Here to Stay • Judith • Nice to Know You • Nookie • One Step Closer • Whatever.
00699744 Book/CD Pack $12.95

5. Funk
Cissy Strut • Cold Sweat, Part 1 • Fight the Power, Part 1 • Flashlight • Pick Up the Pieces • Shining Star • Soul Vaccination • Superstition.
00699745 Book/CD Pack $12.95

6. '90s Rock
Alive • Been Caught Stealing • Cherub Rock • Give It Away • I'll Stick Around • Killing in the Name • Shine • Smells Like Teen Spirit.
00699746 Book/CD Pack $14.99

7. Punk Rock
All the Small Things • Brain Stew (The Godzilla Remix) • Buddy Holly • Dirty Little Secret • Fat Lip • Flavor of the Weak • Lifestyles of the Rich and Famous • Self Esteem.
00699747 Book/CD Pack $14.99

8. '80s Rock
Cult of Personality • Heaven's on Fire • Rock of Ages • Shake Me • Smokin' in the Boys Room • Talk Dirty to Me • We're Not Gonna Take It • You Give Love a Bad Name.
00699832 Book/CD Pack $12.95

9. Big Band
Christopher Columbus • Corner Pocket • Flying Home • In the Mood • Opus One • Stompin' at the Savoy • Take the "A" Train • Woodchopper's Ball.
00699833 Book/CD Pack $12.99

10. blink-182
Adam's Song • All the Small Things • Dammit • Feeling This • Man Overboard • The Rock Show • Stay Together for the Kids • What's My Age Again?
00699834 Book/CD Pack $14.95

Prices, contents and availability subject to change without notice and may vary outside the US.

11. Jimi Hendrix Experience: Smash Hits
All Along the Watchtower • Can You See Me? • Crosstown Traffic • Fire • Foxey Lady • Hey Joe • Manic Depression • Purple Haze • Red House • Remember • Stone Free • The Wind Cries Mary.
00699835 Book/CD Pack $16.95

12. The Police
Can't Stand Losing You • De Do Do Do, De Da Da Da • Don't Stand So Close to Me • Every Breath You Take • Every Little Thing She Does Is Magic • Spirits in the Material World • Synchronicity II • Walking on the Moon.
00700268 Book/CD Pack $14.99

13. Steely Dan
Deacon Blues • Do It Again • FM • Hey Nineteen • Josie • My Old School • Reeling in the Years.
00700202 Book/CD Pack $16.99

14. The Doors
Break on Through to the Other Side • Hello, I Love You (Won't You Tell Me Your Name?) • L.A. Woman • Light My Fire • Love Me Two Times • People Are Strange • Riders on the Storm • Roadhouse Blues.
00699887 Book/CD Pack $14.95

15. Lennon & McCartney
Back in the U.S.S.R. • Day Tripper • Drive My Car • Get Back • A Hard Day's Night • Paperback Writer • Revolution • Ticket to Ride.
00700271 Book/CD Pack $14.99

17. Nirvana
About a Girl • All Apologies • Come As You Are • Dumb • Heart Shaped Box • In Bloom • Lithium • Smells like Teen Spirit.
00700273 Book/CD Pack $14.95

18. Motown
Ain't Too Proud to Beg • Dancing in the Street • Get Ready • How Sweet It Is (To Be Loved by You) • I Can't Help Myself (Sugar Pie, Honey Bunch) • Sir Duke • Stop! in the Name of Love • You've Really Got a Hold on Me.
00700274 Book/CD Pack $12.99

19. Rock Band: Modern Rock Edition
Are You Gonna Be My Girl • Black Hole Sun • Creep • Dani California • In Bloom • Learn to Fly • Say It Ain't So • When You Were Young.
00700707 Book/CD Pack $14.95

20. Rock Band: Classic Rock Edition
Ballroom Blitz • Detroit Rock City • Don't Fear the Reaper • Gimme Shelter • Highway Star • Mississippi Queen • Suffragette City • Train Kept A-Rollin'.
00700708 Book/CD Pack $14.95

21. Weezer
Beverly Hills • Buddy Holly • Dope Nose • Hash Pipe • My Name Is Jonas • Pork and Beans • Say It Ain't So • Undone – The Sweater Song.
00700959 Book/CD Pack $14.99

24. Pink Floyd – Dark Side of the Moon
Any Colour You Like • Brain Damage • Breathe • Eclipse • Money • Time • Us and Them.
00701612 Book/CD Pack $14.99

27. Modern Worship
Beautiful One • Days of Elijah • Hear Our Praises • Holy Is the Lord • How Great Is Our God • I Give You My Heart • Worthy Is the Lamb • You Are Holy (Prince of Peace).
00701921 Book/CD Pack $12.99

FOR MORE INFORMATION,
SEE YOUR LOCAL MUSIC DEALER,
OR WRITE TO:

HAL•LEONARD® CORPORATION
7777 W. BLUEMOUND RD. P.O. BOX 13819
MILWAUKEE, WISCONSIN 53213

Visit Hal Leonard Online at
www.halleonard.com

0511

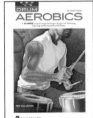